The
Secret
of
Priest's
Grotto

This book is dedicated to the memory of Esther Stermer, author of the book *We Fight to Survive*.

This book is also dedicated to the Stermer, Dodyk, Reible, Goldberg and Kittner families. While many perished in their valiant fight to survive the Holocaust, these brave individuals remind us that human beings are capable of achieving extraordinary things in the face of seemingly insurmountable adversity, fueled by equal parts loyalty and love of family.

–Peter Lane Taylor and Christos Nicola

Kar-Ben Publishing
A division of Lerner Publishing Group, Inc.
241 First Avenue North
Minneapolis, MN 55401 U.S.A.

Website address: www.lernerbooks.com

Library of Congress Cataloging-in-Publication Data

Taylor, Peter Lane.
    The secret of Priest's Grotto / by Peter Lane Taylor with Christos Nicola.
        p.   cm.
    ISBN-13: 978–1–58013–260–2 (lib. bdg. : alk. paper)
    ISBN-10: 1–58013–260–X (lib. bdg. : alk. paper)
    1. Jews—Ukraine—History—20th century—Juvenile literature. 2. Holocaust, Jewish (1939-1945)—Ukraine—Personal narratives—Juvenile literature.
3. Holocaust survivors—Ukraine—Biography—Juvenile literature.
4. Caves—Ukraine—Juvenile literature. 5. Ukraine—Ethnic relations—Juvenile literature. I. Nicola, Christos. II. Title.
DS135.U4T39 2007
940.53'180922477—dc22   2006021709

Manufactured in the United States of America
2 3 4 5 6 –DP– 12 11 10 09 08 07

Photographs © 2007 by Peter Lane Taylor: front cover, back cover (right), pp. 4–5, 5 (right), 6, 8, 9, 10, 13 (left), 14, 16 (left, bottom right), 21, 26, 31, 34, 36, 37, 40, 41 (both), 42 (both), 43 (both), 51 (left), 52, 53, 55 , 57 (left three top row), 62 (bottom right), 63 (top right and bottom right).

Photographs © 2007 by Christos Nicola: pp. 7, 11, 12, 13 (right), 16 (top right), 25, 28 (bottom), 57 (right three top row).

Photographs © 2007 by Steve Duncan: pp. 3, 32, 44, 47, 51 (right).

Courtesy of the Stermer family: back cover (left), pp. front end sheet, 16 (bottom left), 17, 19, 18, 24, 56 (both), 57 (left four bottom row), 58 (left), 59, 61, 62 (top left and bottom middle), 63 (bottom left), rear end sheet.

Courtesy of Sol Wexler: p. 28 (top), 35, 57 (bottom right).

Other photographs used with permission of: © National Archives (W&C 989), p. 23; © United States Holocaust Memorial Museum, pp. 27, 48 (both), 62 (top right); © CORBIS, pp. 29 (left), 46; © DURAND PATRICK/CORBIS-SYGMA, p. 33; © Al Belon/Geophysicial Institute, University of Alaska, p. 39; © Bettmann/CORBIS, p. 49; © Getty Images, p. 50; © dpa/CORBIS, p. 58 (right).

Maps on pp. 22 & 45 © Bill Hauser, Independent Picture Service.

The Secret of PRIEST'S GROTTO

A Holocaust Survival Story

Peter Lane Taylor
with Christos Nicola

KAR-BEN
PUBLISHING
Minneapolis

AMID THE ENDLESS WHEAT FIELDS STRETCHING

ACROSS THE WESTERN UKRAINE, there is a weedy hole in the ground. The only sign of cover for miles around is a low stand of hardwoods,

withering in the heat a short distance away. With the exception of the sinkhole, there is nothing to indicate that one of the longest horizontal labyrinths in the world lies just underfoot.

ON THE AFTERNOON OF JULY 18, 2003, Chris Nicola, a

leading American caver, and Peter Lane Taylor, a caver, writer, and photographer, are standing at the bottom of the shallow depression. It has taken Nicola and Taylor four days of traveling by jet, train, and finally oxcart to journey here from New York City.

In addition to the usual caving paraphernalia, they have brought along 250 pounds (113 kilograms) of photographic equipment and enough supplies to survive underground for three days.

Overhead, the blue sky is rimmed with cumulus clouds sheared off at the top. It is tornado season on the Ukrainian plateau, and their guides are anxious to get the group and all their gear down into the cave.

Cave guides Sergey Yepephanov (left) and Sasha Zimels (right) stand next to caver Chris Nicola and the 30-foot (9 meter) metal entrance pipe that has been installed to provide underground access to Priest's Grotto.

The Ukraine's "Gypsum Giant" cave systems are like nothing else on Earth. Due to its unusual crystalline structure, gypsum fractures at precise geometric angles as it breaks down into cave passages, producing a signature gridlike architecture that propagates outward horizontally like the pattern of hairline cracks across a shattered car windshield. Seven of these enormous labyrinths—amounting to 340 miles (550 kilometers) of contiguous passage and including the 170-mile (270 km) Optimist Cave, the second longest in the world—stretch in all directions beneath the rolling countryside south of Kiev.

Gypsum crystals fracture at precise angles as they break down, forming intricate, mazelike

Taylor has come here to explore the cave for the first time. For Nicola, a twenty-year caving veteran, the expedition is the culmination of a much longer journey that began in 1993, when he became one of the first Americans to explore the Ukraine's caves after the fall of the Soviet Union. On that trip, he explored three of the Gypsum Giants and met dozens of local cavers eager to share news about their recent discoveries. His last excursion was here, to the Priest's Grotto, a cave known officially as Ozernaya, but locally called Popowa Yama. At 77 miles (124 km), Popowa Yama is the second longest of the Gypsum Giants and ranks as the ninth-longest cave in the world.

What brought Nicola back to Priest's Grotto was not the fascinating physical characteristics of the cave, however. It was the fragments of an incredible story that may have taken place in this cave.

On an earlier trip, Nicola's guides took him to a section of the cave called Khatki, or "little cottage," where they encountered two partially intact stone walls and other signs of human habitation, including old shoes, buttons, and a hand-chiseled millstone. Nicola's guides from the local caving association told him that the site had been settled by a group of local Jews who fled to the cave during the Holocaust. But that's where the story ended. By the time the first expeditions into the cave, in 1963, discovered the area where the campsite was located, there was no one alive who could remember what had actually happened there—or even if the Jews had survived the war at all.

Intrigued, Nicola began asking questions in nearby towns. Western Ukraine is a region where the Gypsum

Caver Nicola prepared carefully for his explorations of the Ukraine's underground cave system known as the Gypsum Giants.

Giants have long been revered as national landmarks and the legacy of the Holocaust still lingers uncomfortably close to the surface. Some local villagers told Nicola they saw a group of people covered in thick yellow mud stumbling back to town after the Russians arrived at the end of World War II. Others said the Jews disappeared into the cave but were never seen again.

Nicola's expedition team interviews a local woman from the western Ukrainian town of Korolowka who remembers rumors of the Jews' amazing survival story.

Back in New York, the full magnitude of the Popowa Yama story Nicola had heard from his Ukrainian guide began to hit home. Over the next few years, he returned to the cave several times to expand his investigation into the story, following up on several promising leads. But every one of them turned into a dead end.

Then, on a trip back to the Ukraine in 1997, Nicola met a local caver named Yosef Zimels, who claimed to have escorted a Jewish family from Canada to the sinkhole in 1991 in an attempt to get them inside. According to the caver's story, the family told Zimels they had lived in the grotto with a number of other families during the last two years of the war. All of them were fleeing deportation to the Nazi death

The western Ukrainian village of Bilche-Zolote serenely nestles over an underground landscape that includes some of the longest caves in the world.

camps from their villages of Korolowka and Bilche-Zolote. In all, their group numbered thirty-eight people, including a two-year-old boy and a seventy-five-year-old grandmother, and they had survived in Popowa Yama for nearly a year.

Although he had no reason to doubt the man's story, Nicola could not believe what he had heard. If Zimels's account was accurate and if there were survivors still alive to substantiate the story, it would mean that the world's ninth-longest cave had been discovered not by an elite team of underground explorers but by an ordinary group of Jewish villagers just fighting for their lives. Even more extraordinary, if any of those thirty-eight survivors had stayed inside Popowa Yama for the entire time, they would have exceeded by many months the "official" record of 205 days for the longest period of time any human being has ever spent underground. This record was set by Frenchman Michel Siffre on a 1972 NASA-sponsored long-duration spaceflight experiment in Texas's Midnight Cave.

Nicola's website is that of the Ukrainian American Youth Caver Exchange Foundation, and anyone searching for information on caves in the Ukraine would be likely to be directed there.

Over the next six months, Nicola refocused his investigation on finding a survivor, turning ultimately to the Internet for clues. In the search code for his website on Ukrainian caves (www.uaycef.org), he embedded the words, "Jews," "Holocaust," "western Ukraine," "caves," and "survivors" with the hope that anyone searching the Internet for information about the Popowa Yama story would find his site and contact him. Nothing happened, and the story gradually lost its allure for Nicola as he focused his attention on a series of new and exciting caving expeditions around the world.

Four years later, however, in December 2002, Nicola was hunched over his computer keyboard in his Queens apartment checking his e-mail. It had been over a year since he had been back to the western Ukraine—or even thought about the Popowa Yama story.

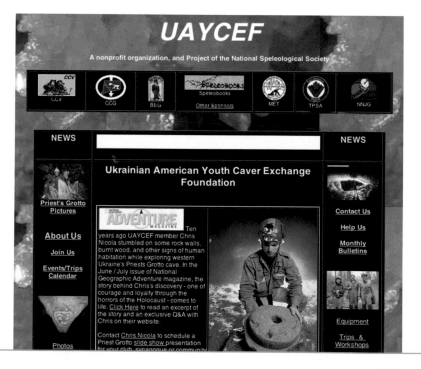

"I hadn't checked my e-mail in a while and there were forty-four messages in my in-box," Nicola remembers vividly of that night. "Usually there's a lot of junk in there so I just started deleting them methodically."

At message forty-three, Nicola stopped suddenly. His eyes widened and his pulse quickened. On the screen, the header of the message read: "Western Ukraine Holocaust Cave Survivor."

The e-mail was from a man named Ed Vogel in nearby Brighton Beach, who wrote that his father-in-law, Sol Wexler, was one of the original thirty-eight survivors from Popowa Yama. Wexler was living by himself just down the block from Vogel. And there were other survivors, he said, living in Florida and Canada. Would Nicola be interested in meeting for coffee or dinner?

From that time on, the Popowa Yama story took over Nicola's life. For the past two years, Nicola had been talking with fellow caver Peter Lane Taylor about writing and photographing an article on the Ukrainian caves. If this story turned out to be true, this would be the article the two men had dreamed about.

Chris Nicola with Priest's Grotto survivor Sol Wexler, right.

Two weeks later, Nicola's initial meeting with Sol Wexler revealed more than he could have imagined, as the first-known Priest's Grotto survivor recounted stories of unprecedented survival, sacrifice, and loyalty. At the end of their meeting, Wexler urged Nicola to contact his cousins—the Stermers—in Montreal, many of whom were also Priest's Grotto survivors.

Over the next five months, Nicola and Taylor took five separate trips to Montreal to meet the extended Stermer family face-to-face. The two quickly discovered that the truth of the Ukrainian cavers' original story was even greater than the myths.

Between 1943 and 1944, three ordinary Jewish families—the Stermers, the Dodyks, and the Kurzs—had survived the Nazi occupation through extraordinary means, living in two different caves, surviving off the land, and running supply lines at night like well-trained military guerrillas.

As Nicola and Taylor learned more about the details of the Jews' survival, the more they realized how unique the story was. The Stermers had faced every possible risk factor—extreme weather, isolation, starvation, persecution—and prevailed. And unlike explorers and adventurers trained in advance to pull themselves back from the brink, there was nothing in these families' pasts that might have prepared them for the ordeal they were about to face. Modern cavers require special clothing to ward off hypothermia, high technology for lighting and travel, and special training in ropes and navigation to survive underground for just a few days. How did thirty-eight untrained, unequipped people—including elderly women and young children—survive for so long in such a hostile environment during history's darkest era?

After lowering down more than 250 pounds (113 kg) of photographic equipment, Peter Lane Taylor descends the 30-foot (9 m) rusty metal shaft that leads into the entry passage of Priest's Grotto.

That was the question Nicola's expedition had now come some 7,000 miles (11,300 km) to answer.

In the early 1960s the entrance into Priest's Grotto was basically a shaft lined with wooden logs, much like that of a well. In the early 1980s, because the shaft continually collapsed following the annual spring snowmelt, the local cavers inserted three 6.5 foot (2 m) long gas pipes (all welded together) in order to prevent further collapses. A similar section was added in mid-1992 so that the accumulating soil in the sinkhole would not bury the opening.

At four thirty in the afternoon, Sergey Yepephanov, the expedition's chief guide, sticks his arm through the steel plate at the top of the vertical entrance pipe and swings open the trapdoor like a manhole cover into some sub-city abyss. Inside the rusty shaft, two dozen rickety metal rungs spot-welded to the inside of the pipe disappear into the darkness, leaving just enough room for each man—and all two dozen of their gear bags—to squeeze down inside of the cave. When Taylor reaches the bottom, he can still make out Sergey's silhouette at the top of the ladder, rimmed by bright, white light.

Seconds later,
Sergey reaches through the small access port,
slams the door to the cave shut,
and everything goes black.

We are not going to go to the slaughterhouse.' She said to my brother Nissel, 'Go into the forest, find a hole, any place. But we are not going there.' Nissel was the oldest son, loyal to the family, and thanks to him, we survived."

Shulim Stermer leaned forward across the dining room table as he spoke, his eyes wide through heavy prescription glasses. His brother Shlomo, their sister Etka Katz, and niece Pepkale Dodyk sat respectfully on either side of him, surrounded by Shulim's wife Czarna, Shlomo's wife Bella, and various children and grandchildren. At eighty-three, Shulim was the oldest-living survivor from Popowa Yama and the undisputed head of the extended Stermer clan. It was July 2003, and at the insistence of Shulim's and Shlomo's cousin Sol Wexler, Nicola and Taylor were in Montreal for a second time to meet with the Stermers and learn more about their family's story.

When Shulim greeted his visitors at the door, he was dressed in a pressed golf shirt and shorts, slippers, and tube socks pulled up high over his calves. He was small and refined and exuded a gentle wisdom that put both guests immediately at ease. His brother Shlomo and sister Etka stood just behind him, smiling warmly.

The Stermers' ninth-floor apartment was spacious and airy, with high ceilings and 8-foot (2.4 m) plate glass windows running the

CLOCKWISE FROM TOP:
Shulim and Shlomo Stermer,
Etka Katz, Nissel Stermer

length of the western wall. The centerpiece of the apartment was a large black-and-white photograph of the six Stermer children with their parents, Esther and Zeida, taken a few years before World War II. In the photo, the Stermers' faces are grave, as if, after the pogroms of the 1890s and Ukrainian famine of 1930, no one was really sure if they'd be around the next time someone had a camera. On the dining room table lay one of their most precious family treasures: a memoir of their survival entitled *We Fight to Survive*, originally written by Esther in Yiddish and privately published in English in 1973.

The Stermer clan: *(from left)* Nissel, Chana, Esther, Shlomo, Zeida, Shulim, Henia Dodyk, Fishel Dodyk, Shunkale Dodyk, and Etka

"My mother never trusted authority," Shulim continued. "The Germans, Russians, the Ukrainians. It didn't matter. She taught us early on that no matter who it was, if they told you to do one thing, you always did the opposite. If the Germans said go to the ghettoes, you'll be safe there, you went to the forest or the mountains. . . . You went as far away from the ghettoes as you could go."

That afternoon the group talked for five hours around Shulim's dining room table about the Stermers' fateful decision to flee underground and how they had managed to survive. In the early 1930s, Esther Stermer was the proud matriarch of one of the most well-regarded families in Korolowka, and her husband Zeida was a successful local merchant. Of their three boys, Nissel was the oldest, followed by Shulim and Shlomo. The three girls were Henia, Chana, and Etka. For many eastern European Jews, it was a rare time of opportunity, and in towns and cities across the Polish Ukraine, Jewish cultural life and Zionism were thriving.

In June 1941, when Hitler's armies stormed across the border from Poland, all that optimism came to a crushing end. Over the next year, Jews across eastern Europe were divested of their property, stripped of their rights, and driven into exile from towns

A 1922 photograph of Esther and her family in happier times *(left to right)*: Nissel, Esther's husband Zeida, holding Shulim, Esther, Chana and Henia. Etka and Shlomo were not born yet.

where their families had lived for hundreds of years. Some managed to flee to larger cities, though most were sent to death camps.

The killings reached Korolowka in the fall of 1942. The town was officially declared *Judenfrei*—"free of Jews"—and the deportations grew more widespread and more systematic. During the Jewish holiday of Sukkot, the Gestapo encircled the town and forced Jews onto conveys destined for the concentration camps. In the weeks that followed, other Jews were forced to dig their own graves before being executed. Esther's memoir recounts some victims still being alive, sticking their heads up through the soil and gasping for air as the Germans walked away. As news of additional executions poured in, the Stermers realized the inevitable: no one would get out alive.

"THE WORLD HAD TURNED ANIMAL— OR WORSE. Every day conditions became worse. Death stalked each step . . . But we were not surrendering to this fate. Our family in particular would not let the Germans have their way easily. We had vigor, ingenuity, and determination to survive. Above all our family would stand together. . . But where could we go? CLEARLY, THERE WAS NO PLACE FOR US ON EARTH."

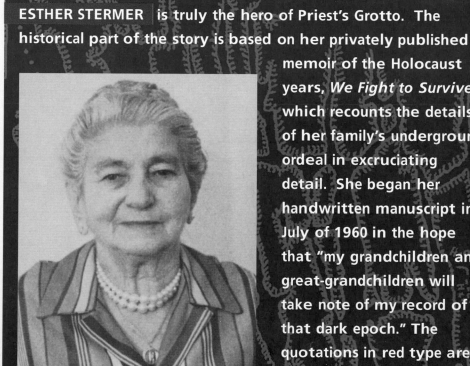

ESTHER STERMER **is truly the hero of Priest's Grotto. The historical part of the story is based on her privately published memoir of the Holocaust years, *We Fight to Survive*, which recounts the details of her family's underground ordeal in excruciating detail. She began her handwritten manuscript in July of 1960 in the hope that "my grandchildren and great-grandchildren will take note of my record of that dark epoch." The quotations in red type are all from Esther's book**

It's already past dinnertime

IT'S ALREADY PAST DINNERTIME when Nicola, Taylor, Sergey, and Sergey's assistant guide Sasha Zimels reach camp, 400 yards (370 m) from the entrance. Although unimpressive in terms of distance, hauling twelve man-days of supplies through Popowa Yama's passageways is no small feat. The cave's tunnels are low and uneven, forcing the men to crouch down and drag their duffels through the mud on their hands and knees. Despite the cave's constant 50°F (10°C) temperature, they all are sweating from the exertion.

The team's camp is a large diamond-shaped chamber that has been used for over a decade by teams making deep explorations into Popowa Yama. There are a dozen smaller bivouac sites scattered strategically throughout the cave's 77 miles (124 km) and the number keeps growing as new passages are discovered. For cavers, these encampments serve the same purpose as advanced alpine camps for mountaineers. Push teams stage themselves between bivouacs during deep multiweek penetrations to keep food and water in constant resupply and maintain their lines of communication with the surface.

To put their current location in context with the rest of the cave, Sergey uses his finger to draw a rough map of the expedition's surroundings in the mud floor.

"We're right here," he explains, pressing his finger into the dense clay. "And this is the entrance to the cave," he goes on, sticking his finger in the mud again, 4 inches (10 centimeters) away. Next, he draws a zigzagging line leading 3 inches (8 cm) straight up to another dot. "This is Khatki," he says, "Where the Jews were during the war."

Sergey then gets up and takes one large step backward to a spot on the floor about 3 feet (1 m) away. "Right here," he says smiling, "is the farthest point we've reached in the cave. That was last year."

Nicola and Taylor look at each other with dawning understanding of why the first cave explorers to find the remains of the Jews' camp didn't grasp the ramifications of what they had discovered. In Khatki the explorers saw little more than a place that humans had already been. They most likely spent a few hours surveying and mapping the area and then quickly moved on to the next virgin section of cave.

That night, Taylor lies awake in his sleeping bag staring wide-eyed into the darkness, seeing all around him the Stermers' faces as they looked in the portrait in Shulim's apartment. Was it true what Shulim had said the first day they met his family: "Everyone has it inside of them to survive"? Taylor wondered if he would be capable of the same will to fight for his own family's survival.

Ukrainian cave guides Sasha Zimels (left) *and Sergey Yepephanov* (right) *rest in a basecamp called "Kama" used by modern explorers.*

when the Stermers and their neighbors finally ran for good, was dark and unseasonably cold. The roads in and out of Korolowka were empty of the usual cart traffic that peaked during harvesttime. After a month of backbreaking work, most residents were already drifting off to sleep.

At just before midnight, the Stermers dug up the last of their remaining possessions, which they had buried behind their house, loaded their wagons, and fled north along with eighteen other Jews. Their destination was a well-known tourist cave called Verteba, the first of two underground refuges they would inhabit during the war. Verteba was located half an hour outside of Bilche-Zolote by foot or horse-drawn cart, and with heavy winter snows just weeks away, the 4.8-mile (8 km) cave would be deserted until spring.

The Stermers' decision to take refuge underground was a radical move, despite a history of subterranean human habitation throughout the area and in Verteba in particular. Most Jewish families fighting to survive Hitler's Final Solution divided themselves into small groups between safe houses and bunkers in the forest, hoping that at least one family member would live to carry on the bloodline. Others disbanded altogether to live off the land like scavengers. The Stermers decided instead to bet on one another.

"We knew that we had a better chance of survival sticking together," Pepkale said. "We knew that our family would always be loyal to one another . . . Even when things were at their worst, you could always look around and see your sister,

The Priest's Grotto and Verteba caves are located in the western Ukraine. In 1942, they lay directly in the path of Hitler's march to Stalingrad and the Black Sea.

Allies

Greater Germany and Occupied Territories

German Allies or Dependant States

Neutral

0   100 MI

your mother, and the rest of your family. It helped us to remember what we were fighting for."

After squeezing in through the narrow entrance, the group turned right and quickly found themselves in an area of the cave where few humans had ever been before. In their first few hours underground, the darkness around them must have seemed immeasurable. Navigating with only candles and lanterns, they would have had no depth perception and would have been unable to see farther than a few feet into the distance.

For their home, the survivors chose a natural alcove approximately 40 feet (12 m) across, which they were able to enclose with a hastily constructed rock wall. Once settled, they gravely considered what to do next. Despite the physical protection the cave offered, Verteba was a temporary refuge at best. The would-be survivors had no weapons or long-term supplies, there was no natural water source, and because of the cave's relatively short length, they would almost certainly be discovered when the snows melted in April and tourists began coming back to the cave.

"WE KNEW THAT OUR FAMILY WOULD ALWAYS BE LOYAL TO ONE ANOTHER. . . . Even when things were at their worst, you could always look around and see your sister, your mother, and the rest of your family. IT HELPED US TO REMEMBER WHAT WE WERE FIGHTING FOR."

The love and loyalty that existed among the family members were their sole weapon against the highly organized, well-trained troops of the Nazi regime.

Through the winter of 1942-1943, the Jews' survival hung in a precarious balance between the secrecy of their location and the security of their supply lines, which were faithfully maintained by Zeida, Nissel, and Pepkale's father Fishel Dodyk. Prior to fleeing to Verteba, the three men had received special permission to collect scrap metal under official protection from the local police. It was perilous, humiliating labor. But their ability to move freely in public and buy supplies on the black market represented their family's only lifeline to the surface. Every week, they drove their wagons to the cave under cover of darkness through the deep snow and subzero winds. At the edge of the sinkhole, they descended the steep icy slopes carrying 100-pound (45 kilogram) sacks of flour, potatoes, kerosene, and water on their backs and then dragged the supplies through the mud inside of the cave. Nissel, Zeida, and Fishel are now deceased, and without their firsthand testimonies, it's impossible to imagine the horrors they endured to keep their families alive during those long winter months. Week after week, they repeated their supply runs without fail and then returned to Korolowka to live as outcasts in a world that was bent on their destruction.

"Nissel was our most important contact with the outside world," Esther wrote of her oldest son. "Every trip (he) made outside was an odyssey more hazardous than anything the Greeks ever dreamed of in their nightmares. . . . Those who have been spared our tribulations can hardly imagine how much courage, ingenuity, strength, and determination his daily activities called for."

Esther's son Nissel in 1936. He had been in the Polish Cavalry before being branded a Jew and forced into being a scrap metal collector.

"ALL THIS TIME, WE DID NOT SEE DAYLIGHT OR THE SUN'S RAYS. . . . The air in the outside world was poisoned by Nazism which spurred all peoples to kill as many of the surviving Jews as they could. EVEN ABOVE THE GROTTO THERE WAS NO SUNSHINE FOR THE PURSUED PERSECUTED JEWS."

Nissel, Zeida, and Fishel also brought with them news from the outside. The terror against the Ukrainian Jewry was increasing daily, and as spring approached, the Gestapo would resume their hunt for Jews hiding in the forest. It was only a matter of time, the men warned, before their refuge inside Verteba would be discovered.

"Our situation at that time was really, really bad. . . ." Shlomo finally said, rubbing his palms on his knees nervously as he spoke. "We didn't have any water, and we had to catch the drips that came off the walls in cups. We also couldn't cook inside without choking on the smoke . . . We had no idea how we were going to survive."

Next to him, Shulim listened quietly and put his hands together on his lap in a way that suggested he was praying. In the awkward silence that followed, we realized that we had arrived at one of the lowest points in the Stermers' story.

In early February 1943, with no other way to survive in or outside of Verteba, the Jews decided to move deeper into the cave to areas where no human had ever been before. They sealed themselves in a low sickle-shaped room more than 3,000 feet (900 m) from daylight and began to search frantically for a second secret exit in case the Gestapo attempted to blockade them inside. Shulim, Shlomo, and Nissel discovered a small fracture in the ceiling of a nearby passage and feverishly began digging upward, carving steps into walls to keep their balance in the narrow shaft. Four weeks later, the men finally broke through to the surface, many of them seeing the sunset for the first time in five months.

Before returning underground, Shulim concealed their exit and suspended a long chain down to the cave's floor below. If the Nazis discovered their refuge, his family could escape through the secret exit by climbing up the chain like a rope and using the kick steps for support. After

(From left) Bella Stermer (wife of Shlomo), Pepkale Dodyk, Shlomo Stermer, Erin Grunstein (grand-daughter of Shulim), Lila Stermer (daughter of Shlomo), Shulim Stermer, and Czarna (wife of Shulim).

roughly 150 days of living in perpetual terror of being discovered, the Stermers and their neighbors finally began to feel like their chances of surviving were improving.

The exact details of what happened next remain unclear even today. The survivors had been sleeping for almost eighteen hours when the Gestapo stormed their refuge, and in the chaos that followed, it was impossible for anyone to distinguish between what was real and what was a nightmare.

Chris Nicola and Mikael Sohtasky examine and survey what remains of the survivors' second encampment inside of Verteba cave.

"The Germans are here!" someone suddenly yelled in Yiddish, "They've discovered us!"

Shlomo was sleeping close to the entrance of the chamber and was caught helpless before he had the chance to run. In the glare of the Gestapo's flashlights, he could see that others had been captured too, including his sister Henia and her daughter Pepkale, Esther's sister Leiche and her sons Sol and Lonchia, and Usher Metzger. Sleeping farther inside the sickle-shaped passageway, the rest of the Stermer children quickly slipped away into the darkness. At the entrance to their refuge, Shlomo could hear his mother Esther standing toe-to-toe with the Nazis' commanding officer and speaking German.

" 'Very well, so you have found us. What do you think?' my mother said slowly, 'Do you think that unless you kill us the Fuehrer will lose the war? Look at how we live here, like rats. All we want is to live, to survive the war years. Leave us here.' "

Shlomo leaned forward over the dining room table and rose out of his chair to imitate his mother as he spoke. "I couldn't believe what I was hearing!" he continued. "Here was my mother, in the middle of the war, standing up to the Germans!"

As Esther confronted the soldiers, stalling for time, the rest of her children and the other survivors crawled away into the dark maze of passageways branching off from the campsite. When she was done, only eight of the Jews were taken prisoner and marched back toward the cave's entrance at gunpoint. But miraculously along the way, three of them, including Esther and Shlomo, managed to break away into the darkness before the

Hitler die letzte Rettung

Darum: Her zu uns!

Somehow, through the courage of her convictions and the love of her family, Esther was able to stand up to the Nazi regime and all it stood for.

"DO YOU THINK THAT UNLESS YOU KILL US THE FUEHRER WILL LOSE THE WAR? Look at how we live here, like rats. All we want is to live, **to survive the war years.** LEAVE US HERE."

ABOVE: The Wexler family in Myshkoff, Poland in 1937. The only ones in the photograph to survive the Holocaust were Leiche's husband Munie Wexler (*middle row left*) and their son Sol Wexler (*front row left and* **BELOW**)

soldiers could shoot them. Days later, Henia, Pepkale, Usher Metzger, and Sol Wexler would also escape from the local police and be reunited with their family. Only Sol Wexler's mother Leiche and his brother Lonchia would never be seen again.

For the twenty-three Jews who remained inside the cave, the next several hours were spent in a state of terror and confusion. Few of the survivors had kept track of how far they had fled from the main camp in the dark, and many, like Esther, ended up out of earshot of one another—lost without matches, candles, water, or any idea of how to find their way back to camp.

For Shulim, in particular, the shock of being discovered was devastating. Hours later, when Esther finally found her way back to the encampment, she was horrified to find her middle son lying paralyzed at the bottom of the exit shaft.

"I saw that all had climbed through the exit except Shulim who was sitting on the ground trembling, head thrown back. I ran to him, spoke to him, but he did not reply. His eyes were glazed, his teeth clenched and he was drooling at the mouth."

Back in Montreal, Shulim grew quiet when we broached the topic of his breakdown. Nicola and Taylor already knew that it had taken two months for him to recover completely, and they were wary of agitating old ghosts.

"I was almost destroyed in the first cave," Shulim finally offered, "I had a complete shock. I couldn't talk. . . . I couldn't walk. . . . I couldn't take a spoon and pick it up to my mouth. . . . It was a miracle that I even survived."

For the other Jews who had already reached the top of the exit shaft, it was the worst possible time for Shulim to break down. No one else knew how to open the trapdoor, and they soon began to bottleneck near the surface,

Verteba Cave Occupants

The Stermers: Esther, her unmarried sons Shulim and Shlomo, and her unmarried daughters Chana and Etka

The Dodyks: Esther's daughter Henia and her husband Fishel, and their daughters Shunkale and Pepkale

The Wexlers: Esther's sister Leiche, and her children Sol and Lonchia

The Bodians: his wife, sister, and her fiancé, as well as his parents

The Franks: plus their son and his wife and their daughter and her husband

The Barads: Hersh, his wife and their two children, as well as his mother

Mr. Chisdes, the Hebrew teacher

Esther's husband Zeida and her son Nissel and her son-in-law Fishel Dodyk had permission to collect scrap metal for the Nazis and thus did not need refuge in the cave.

For the Verteba dwellers, escape from the cave just meant facing further dangers, as the Gestapo lay in wait for the fugitives on the surface.

panicked and unable to see who or what was around them. Shulim's sisters Chana and Etka, and Sol Wexler were the first to reach the top. But even with two of them pushing with their arms and heads, they were unable to move the logs that locked the door in place. The situation soon began to get dangerously out of control.

Finally, with one last effort, Sol and Chana succeeded in breaking through to the surface, and everyone rushed from the exit into the tall grass lining the gently sloping hill. Outside, the air was cold and wet, and many of the survivors began to shiver uncontrollably. To the north, they could see the Gestapo and their dogs running search grids around the sinkhole looking for a secret exit. Shulim was the last to leave, carried up the shaft on his brother's shoulders.

Moments later, as the Gestapo continued their search, the survivors slipped away through the grass and fled into the darkness.

The sinkhole leading down to the entrance of Priest's Grotto lies only a few hundred yards from the nearby woods. For the survivors, it seemed like miles as they ran from the cave's entrance to collect firewood and other supplies.

TAYLOR'S WRISTWATCH TELLS HIM it's just past eight in the morning

when he and Nicola wake up from their first night underground. They light their small stove for coffee, rouse Sergey and Sasha, and groggily begin to prepare their carbide lamps and mapping gear for the day's trip to Khatki. After less than twenty-four hours in the cave, both men can already feel the sense of suspended reality that the Stermers told them about in Montreal: with no sunlight to mark the passing hours, everything seems like it's happening in slow motion.

In terms of raw feet, the hike from base camp to Khatki is only about 400 yards (370 m). But in a labyrinth-type cave, the challenge of getting from one place to another is best measured in number of turns rather than linear distance. Unlike most vertical caves, where the greatest risks are from falling and being struck by a rock from overhead, it's the randomness and repetition that kill in caves like Popowa Yama. Every passageway looks the same, and for even the most experienced speleologists, the disorientation of getting lost can quickly escalate into full-blown panic. In the best-case scenarios, victims take one wrong turn and return quickly to their last known location. In the worst cases, cavers get lost in a maze of endless switchbacks without food and water and eventually their lights run out.

Sergey takes Nicola and Taylor on the most direct course to Khatki, navigating the entire way from memory without a map or compass. Their route redirects itself left, right, and backward over increasingly uneven ground exactly sixteen times before they finally arrive at a round natural archway where local cavers have erected a mud sign overhead identifying the historic area's entrance.

This skeleton, found by Nicola in a nearby gypsum cave, is believed to be that of a Ukrainian rebel or bandito who lost his way in the labyrinth.

To make sure Nicola and Taylor can find their way back to camp later in the day, Sergey flags their route every 10 to 15 feet (3 to 5 m) with pink survey tape and points out the cave's most significant landmarks.

"In caves like Popowa Yama, you don't need to pay a guide to get you in," Sergey likes to joke. "You pay me to show you the way back out."

NO OTHER MAN has pioneered the field of human isolation as Michel Siffre has. He collectively has spent more time underground than anyone else on Earth. The Frenchman called his early experiences with sensory deprivation "living beyond time," and in each of his long-term isolation "experiments" dating back to 1962, the loneliness and monotony of life underground drove him insane.

"After 63 days of numbing cold, constant dampness, and almost unbearable stress," he wrote of his first prolonged confinement in the French-Italian Maritime Alps, "I emerged as a half-crazed disjointed marionette."

In 1972 in Texas's Midnight Cave, where Siffre set the last modern record for time underground, not even a half million dollars worth of sophisticated equipment and a panel of scientists monitoring him could prevent his eventual breakdown. On day 79, Siffre called the surface pleading, "J'en ai marre!—I've had enough!" By day 163, his mental and manual dexterity had deteriorated so acutely that he could do little more with his time than study the movements of a mouse.

"I am living through the nadir of my life," he wrote. "Two ideas obsess me: I am wasting my life in this stupid research; I must get out of Midnight Cave now! My thoughts . . . unfold with singular logic and lucidity. Actually, my mind has temporarily collapsed."

To understand the Stermers' accomplishment inside of Priest's Grotto, consider the following: by the time Siffre exited Midnight Cave, after 205 days underground, the Priest's Grotto survivors were barely two-thirds of the way through their own underground internment. Since Siffre's last experiment, no one has attempted to repeat his underground experiment or break his record.

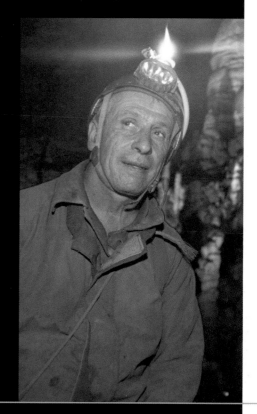

Michel Siffre's 205 days underground is the official world record—but unofficially that record belongs to the Stermers.

Through the first two weeks of April 1943, the survivors lived like condemned prisoners in their own community. They moved along the back roads at night between the boarded-up remains of their house and an attic bunker in a barn outside Bilche-Zolote. Virtually everything they once owned had been looted or burned when the Gestapo drove them out of their camp in Verteba.

Desperate to find a permanent refuge, Nissel went to visit his Ukrainian friend Munko Lubudzin, a local forester who lived in the woods outside of Korolowka and had faithfully sold the Stermers supplies throughout the war. Munko told Nissel about

The original entrance to Priest's Grotto, first discovered by the Stermer and Dodyk brothers and a friend named Karl Kurz in spring 1943, is now filled in by debris and overgrown with weeds.

a sinkhole a few miles outside of town named Popowa Yama—the "Priest's Grotto"—because of its location in the fields of a local parish priest. At the surface, there was nothing remarkable about the place. The steep banks of the sinkhole were overgrown with weeds, farmers had thrown their dead livestock into the bottom to rot, and unlike Verteba, there was no indication a cave lay on the other side, except for a series of small cracks in the exposed bedrock where water dripped in.

On May 1, 1943, Nissel, Shulim, Ziundi (Karl) Kurz, and Mendel and Yossel Dodyk (relatives of Fishel Dodyk) set out from Korolowka to see Popowa Yama for themselves.

"When we came there, there was some nice, nice grass, like a golf course," Shulim began, his voice rising excitedly. "Beautiful grass, and you walked down and then you have a big ravine about 40 feet (12 m) deep where water used to drip in."

At the edge of the sinkhole, the men descended the loose dirt using an old rope, then clambered down the last 20 vertical feet (6 m) using several old logs as a makeshift ladder. At the bottom, the mud came up to their knees and the stench of rotting livestock made them gag.

Nissel was the first to squeeze through the narrow opening of the cave. Inside, it was completely dark, but by the dim light of his candle, he could see that he was in a small room surrounded by large boulders. About 75 feet (23 m) farther on, Nissel rose to stand and found himself in a chamber so large his candle could scarcely light the walls or the ceiling overhead. When all five of the men had joined him, they pulled out a coil of rope, tied one end to a boulder, and walked off into the darkness to find a suitable place for camp. Three hours later, disoriented and fatigued, Shulim dragged his foot over a small ledge, dislodging a stone, which rolled downhill into a clear underground lake. The men shined their lights at one another and laughed for the first time in months: they had found water.

"By the time we went into the second cave, I think there was truly no place else that we could go," Pepkale said. "It was Judenfrei. Any Jew who was seen anywhere could have been shot by anybody. We were a large family, one of the few left in the area. . . . I think it was just a Godsend that we found this place."

Priest's Grotto Cave Occupants

Stermer: Zeida and Esther, their sons Nissel, Shulim, and Shlomo, and their unmarried daughters Chana and Etka

Dodyk (1st Group): Fishel (son of Choncia Dodyk) and his wife Henia (daughter of Esther Stermer), and their daughters Shunkale and Pepkale

Kittner: Brothers Shimon and Leib, and Leib's son Shunia

Goldberg: Etcia Goldberg (daughter of Choncia Dodyk), Etcia's daughter Mania (Mariya), and her sons Dunia (Daniel) and Marek

Dodyk (2nd Group): Choncia, her son Mendel, his wife Yetta and their daughter Regina; Choncia's unmarried daughter Fradel; Choncia's son Yossel, his wife Pepcia and their son Nunia (Norman) Kittner, adopted by Kittners after his parents died

Wexler: Sol (nephew of Esther Stermer)

Kurz: Siomo and Karl (nephews of Esther Stermer)

Kavalek: Mayer and Hersch (cousins of Fishel Dodyk)

Reibel: Meimel (daughter of Choncia Dodyk), Meimel's daughters Mania and Dortcia (Dorothy), and sons Mundek (Marvin) and Luzer (Louis)

Barad: Ulo and his sister Frida (nephew and niece of Yetta Dodyk)

Four boys from Priest's Grotto in 1945: *(from left)* Mundek Reibel, Sol Wexler, Luzer Reibel, and Shlomo Stermer.

Five days later, on May 5, Esther and Zeida Stermer, their six children, four other relatives, and twenty-six other Jews packed up their last supplies and fled to Popowa Yama for good. They descended the sinkhole one by one in silence, climbing hand over hand down the rocky face and stepping on the slippery wet logs for support. At the bottom, the darkness emanating from inside the narrow entrance was terrifying, and the youngest children started to cry as they crawled through the rotting cattle carcasses and into the opening. It would be the last time many of them would see the sky for nearly a year.

The survivors chose a series of four interconnected rooms for their new home, far to the left of Popowa Yama's main passageways. Compared to the world they left above them, the initial security of their new refuge must have seemed like heaven. For the

The entrance to Khatki: long, narrow passageways branch off from a single entryway, providing the survivors with separate areas to cook, sleep, eat, and gather for meetings.

smallest children, like three-year-old Pepkale and her eight-year-old sister Shunkale, Popowa Yama was the first taste of real freedom they had ever experienced. The virgin cave was also their own secret discovery. And most important, other than a handful of outside supply contacts, no one else in the world even knew that the Stermers and their neighbors were still alive.

It wasn't long, however, before the families' initial sense of security was overshadowed by the question of how they were going to survive. Drawing on the lessons from Verteba, they found a ventilated chamber to build their cooking fire, isolated their water sources, and quickly turned to reestablishing their supply lines to Bilche-Zolote. With no end to the war in sight, it was impossible to predict how many months or years the survivors would need to stockpile their resources, and there was only enough kerosene, flour, matches, and other supplies remaining to last two weeks. This time, moreover, neither Nissel, Fishel, nor any of the other men would have special permission to perform chores that would exempt them from the killings above. Once they passed through Popowa Yama's entrance, they would be completely on their own.

"We wouldn't be alive today if it weren't for them!" Etka said suddenly.

It was the first time Shulim and Shlomo's sister had spoken all afternoon. But her words had succinctly captured something about the Stermers' story that Nicola and Taylor would come to see as the most remarkable part of their saga: the extent to which they had willingly risked their lives for

"LONG AGO, people believed that spirits and ghosts lived in ruins and in caves. Now we could see that there were none here. THE DEVILS AND THE EVIL SPIRITS WERE ON THE OUTSIDE, NOT IN THE GROTTO."

Chris Nicola crouches by the survivors' main water source.

one another so that their entire family would survive. Whereas many of history's famous survival stories are notable precisely because of their rapacious Darwinism, the Stermers' triumph was proof that sacrifice and selflessness can still compete with guns and steel.

Two weeks later, as the men left Khatki on their first mission outside of the cave, Shulim and his two brothers felt emboldened by this sense of unity and dedication. At the top of the sinkhole, they sprinted through the high grass to the edge of the Yasinovaty woods 1,000 feet (300 m) away, where they crouched down and waited. Overhead, a thin crescent moon lay hidden behind a dark skin of low-flying clouds, and the wind blew across the plains with a persistent moan. From behind the trees, Nissel scanned the horizon to see if anyone had seen them come out of the sinkhole. But the landscape was eerily quiet, a few smoldering buildings the only signs of life.

On Nissel's cue, the men then scattered into the woods and began to cut down twenty large trees, working frantically with axes and saws in almost total darkness. Half of the men chopped off the branches and cut the trunks into 5-foot (1.5 m) lengths, while the others carried the logs back to the cave across the open fields.

"This was really terrible danger," Shulim exclaimed, whispering the last word for emphasis. "You hear. . . . You listen. And you hear the cutting with the axe: 'POW! BOOM! BAM!' So much noise!" As he spoke, Shulim cut his hands through the air in front of him, a sense of defiance still lingering in his voice.

A few nights later, the men ventured outside of the cave again, splitting up at the edge of the sinkhole to secure supplies for their own individual families. Nissel and Shulim sprinted west through the fields toward Bilche-Zolote, staying near the trees for cover and watching the rotation of the stars to keep track of how long they were gone. It was a 4-mile (6 km) roundtrip journey from Popowa Yama to Munko's house, where the brothers traded their last remaining valuables for vital supplies such as cooking oil, detergent, matches, and flour.

"EACH TIME ANYONE LEFT OUR SHELTER, IT WAS TO FACE INSTANT AND CONSTANT DEATH. . . ."

"When we got out, there was the Big Dipper," Shulim told us when we asked how they kept time without watches. "The Big Dipper was like that. . . ." In the empty space in front of him, Shulim circumscribed a wide arc with his arms across the table. "It was turn, turning, turning, and when it was almost horizontal we knew it would soon be morning. We knew that we had to get back."

When Nissel, Shulim, and the other men finally returned to the cave, they whispered a prearranged password to one of the younger boys posted just inside of the entrance, who quickly dislodged a large boulder to let them back in. Once they were safely on the other side, the men collapsed onto the floor in a combination of exhaustion and relief.

"Each time anyone left our shelter," Esther wrote of her sons' trips outside of the cave, "it was to face instant and constant death. . . . I nearly went out of my mind before I saw [my sons'] return. My heart was affected by these constant anxieties and to this day I live on pills."

The next day, as the men slept for twenty uninterrupted hours, Shlomo, Chana, Henia, Sol Wexler, and Esther piled the Stermers' rations neatly under their rough-hewn, wooden bunks, which Shulim had constructed from logs and scrap lumber scavenged from the nearby woods. In all, the men had secured enough supplies for another six weeks.

The position of the stars warned the men the daylight would be coming soon, and they had best take whatever they had been able to scavenge back to the darkness of the cave.

"You won't believe this, Peter!" Nicola yells from out of the

darkness. "The stone walls are still here!"

From the entrance to Khatki where Taylor is staging his photography gear, he can hear the awe and relief in Nicola's voice booming down the passageway. In the months preceding their expedition, they often worried whether Khatki might have been ransacked by vandals or washed clean by the floods that periodically sweep the cave. Instead, the team has discovered what amounts to a near virgin archaeological site. Each of Khatki's four main rooms is approximately 8 feet (2.4 m) wide and between 30 and 50 feet (9 to 15 m) long and linked to the others by a network of narrow body-width tunnels at either end. The rock ceiling is curved and comes down to the floor like a covered wagon. At the back of the entry room, Nicola kneels in the weak orange glow spilling from his carbide headlamp, his arms moving wildly in silhouette against the rocks behind him as he digs through the dirt.

"The walls are leveled at the bottom with rocks," he continues breathlessly. "And there's smoke on the ceiling here. . . . It looks like it leads back here. . . ."

By the time Taylor makes his way to where Nicola was kneeling, he's already gone, through a hidden back passage to the next room, where Sergey has discovered the Stermers' most prized possession: a 150-pound (70-kg) millstone that Nissel stole from a farmer's barn and carried on his back to the cave from over 3 miles (5 km) away. Combined with a solid-rock base hand-chiseled by Shulim with a 6-inch (15-cm) railroad spike, the millstone was used by the survivors to grind flour from grain and was one of their most critical tools.

Chris Nicola examines the survivors' millstone that Nissel Stermer carried on his back from a nearby farm and Shulim Stermer fashioned into use with a chisel and rock hammer. The millstone allowed the Jews to make flour from grain for soup and bread.

The 30-foot-long (9 m) room is completely empty, except for a large pile of rectangular stones lying in the corner. In the crossbeams of our flashlights, the millstone looks as if it's on museum display. Impulsively, Sergey steps forward to pick it up. He puts his hands on the cold sides of the stone and jerks his small but powerful body upward twice. The millstone barely moves from its base.

Past the remains of another artificial wall, we crawl on our hands and knees into the survivors' sleeping quarters. The passage is almost 80 feet (24 m) long and in many places less than 4 feet (1 m) high. On the left as we enter, there's a trench dug down into the earth that allows us to walk half the distance standing almost upright. On the right, the floor is scattered with artifacts, including over a dozen old leather shoes, porcelain buttons, broken ceramics, and, lying overturned in the dirt, a red metal cup etched on the bottom in Yiddish.

For the next three hours, Nicola and Taylor photograph all the objects and map their location while Sergey and Sasha continue to dust around deeper inside the passage, handling each artifact they find as if it were a fragile living species. Collectively, the two Ukrainian guides have spent over five hundred days during the past twenty years mapping the unexplored passageways around us. Yet, today's discoveries have left them speechless at the survivors' endurance and ingenuity. The last three things they uncover before returning to camp for dinner are a front door key, the Stermers' small

The survivors' mug discovered in Priest's Grotto, which matches

The remains of an old leather shoe discovered by Sergey Yepephanov in

6-inch (15 cm) chisel, and a decaying wooden runner from a collapsible sled Shulim built to ferry supplies to the cave through the deep winter snow.

On the way back to camp, Nicola and Taylor wander off course at every turn, disoriented by the magnitude of their discoveries. Like hieroglyphics, the artifacts and their locations have given them a direct physical link to the past and provided proof of the Stermers' title to the longest period of time any human being has ever spent underground.

The shards of a painted ceramic plate discovered by Chris Nicola

An old house key that was carried into the cave by one of the survivors

the entrance to Popowa Yama and the nearby woods remained devoid of people. About 70 feet (21 m) underground, the Stermers and their neighbors lived in a state of near hibernation. Day and night were indistinguishable, and their circadian rhythms quickly became reconfigured for survival. They slept for eighteen to twenty-two hours at a time to conserve energy, lying side by side on hard wooden planks and rising only to eat, go to the bathroom, and attend to the rudiments of staying alive.

With the approach of summer, the survivors began to transform the cave's geology into something suitable for long-term habitation, digging trenches so they could work without hunching over and raising artificial walls to retain their body heat and reduce wind draft. The combination of the cave's naturally humid interior and the moisture from the Jews' own respiration kept their tattered clothes constantly damp, and even the slightest breeze could quickly induce hypothermia.

The Stermers worked in the dark most of the time, not wanting to waste their precious candles. Divisions of labor were unspoken, and the chain of leadership down from Esther and Zeida to their oldest sons was never questioned. "Inside our cave, each one of us did his assigned duties," Esther wrote of their first month underground, "We cooked, we washed, we made needed repairs. Cleanliness was of the utmost importance. Life in our grotto went on with its own normality."

As the High Holidays approached, the group felt they should observe them. Esther writes, "We had a prayer book for the High Holidays. My son-in-law Fishel conducted the services. On the day of Yom Kippur, we fasted and prayed."

A distinct "smoke line" in the rock ceiling establishes the location of the survivors' cooking chamber in Priest's Grotto. If smoke from the survivors' cooking fires did not vent from the cave's passages, there was a risk of asphyxiation and death.

To hedge against the possibility that they might be discovered again, Nissel, Shulim, Shlomo, Fishel Dodyk, and the other men began searching for a place to dig another secret exit. They found they could walk for hours without ever retracing their steps. It is impossible to say for sure how far they traveled back into Popowa Yama's interior. By this time, the men were finely attuned to the state of sensory deprivation underground. They walked barefoot over the uneven rocks in the dark and could recognize the "feel" of each passageway from the Braille-like signature of its walls. They were in command of the place.

In early July, however, the survivors' newfound confidence was shattered by the sound of Mendel Dodyk screaming. "The entrance to the cave is blocked!" he shouted, returning to Khatki, "We will all die here of starvation!"

Fighting off the dampness and confusion, Nissel, Shulim, and the other men jumped from their beds and crawled quickly to the entrance, discovering a wall of earth and rocks trapping them inside. From so far underground, it was impossible to know if some of the men had been spotted in the woods or if a Gestapo patrol had followed their tracks to the entrance. Whoever it was, instead of storming the entrance as at Verteba, they had simply sealed them in.

A few yards (meters) away, the men found a narrow gap between two rocks and frantically started to dig for daylight. For the next three nights, they tunneled upward, chiseling away at the stones as the loose fracture gradually turned toward the ceiling. On the fourth day, Nissel pried a large rock from the

PRIEST'S GROTTO—Khatki section

○ **Junction Room**

1 Entrance to Khakti section of cave

2 The names Stermer, Salomon, Dodyk and K. Kurz are blackened into the ceiling with the year 1943

3 Water source

10m (11y)

4 Sleeping area of the Stermers and Sol Wexler

5 Sleeping area of the Dodyks

6 Sleeping area for the others

···· Indicates route used by survivors

top of the shaft and felt the wind rush in from outside, carrying with it the warm, tangy aroma of a passing thunderstorm. Not long afterward, the survivors learned that a group of Ukrainian villagers had worked for days with picks and shovels until they filled the ravine with rocks and earth and blocked the entrance to the cave.

"Some of the Ukrainians helped us to survive," Shulim said politely, referring to friends such as Munko. "But some of them weren't so nice."

In the days after their discovery, the survivors returned to a state of primal fear, guarding the cave's entrance with sickles and axes and constantly listening for the sound of strange voices. Without a way to get safely to the surface, it was impossible to know whether the Nazis were watching the sinkhole or if they had given the survivors up for dead. Back in Khatki, some of the survivors started to panic. There was very little food and fuel left, and soon the men would have no choice but to go out of the cave for supplies. The importance of finding a second secret exit was now a matter of life and death.

The following day, Nissel, Shulim, Shlomo, and the other men ventured deeper into Popowa Yama's labyrinths than ever before, looking desperately for breaches in the cave's ceiling while marking their routes with pieces of colored string. But the muddy walls were impossible to climb, and to make forward progress through the cave's narrowest corridors, they were constantly moving boulders, digging trenches, and clawing at the earth with their bare hands.

When the men finally found a suitable place two weeks later, Shulim and Nissel began to dig in the cracks between the rocks, working day and night for weeks on end. Beyond 50 feet (15 m), however, their

The Nazis ordered the Ukrainians to aid in the search for Jews in their local communities. Some of them cooperated with the Nazis, while others attempted to help their former friends and neighbors.

The survivors built artificial rock walls in both of their cave locations. The structures served not only to conceal their location but also to retain body heat.

"THIS WAS A TREMENDOUS SETBACK FOR ALL OF US. It is difficult to describe the frustration and labor which we passed through in those days."

route became a combination of sand and gravel on one side and thick blue clay on the other. As they tried to dig higher, the shaft started to collapse along the seam, showering the men with rock and debris. After two serious cave-ins, the men gave up for good.

"This was a tremendous setback for all of us," wrote Esther, "It is difficult to describe the frustration and labor which we passed through in those days."

For the next two months, Nissel, Shulim, Fishel, and the other men risked their lives weekly to maintain the families' tenuous supply lines. During the summer, the fields surrounding Priest's Grotto were busy with Ukrainian farmers tending their crops and livestock, and if any of the Jews were ever caught, the survival of the entire group would be in danger. With the first signs of autumn, the Stermers and the other families refocused their energies on stocking up on food, fuel, tools, and

As much as the Stermers and the other families were suffering underground, they were still better off than those on the surface. There was a full-scale roundup of all Jews underway. **(ABOVE)** Those who survived the capture were shipped in freight cars. **(RIGHT)** And those who survived the freight cars were taken to concentration camps.

blankets for another long winter. Unlike Michel Siffre, whose confinement was catered with filet mignon and Mariott in-flight meals designed for the *Apollo 16* astronauts, every one of the thirty-eight Jews had become dangerously malnourished by this point. Their meager diet of grain and potatoes threatened them with scurvy and jaundice, and without enough protein, calcium, minerals, and vitamins C and D in their diet, the very act of fighting for survival was slowly killing them from within. If they ran out of food during the winter, they would die a slow and certain death from starvation.

Yet, aboveground, the chances of the men being caught—and of the Jews' refuge being discovered—had never been greater. The lack of food and activity had made the men weak, and during harvesttime, the Nazis had stepped up their patrols to find Jews in the woods. For Nissel, Shulim, and the other men, the last two weeks of October were the ultimate test of will and endurance. Aware that potatoes were being dug up and left in big piles in the fields, they knew that this was their last opportunity to bring winter supplies back to the cave. They hid in the attic of a local peasant during the days, scarcely eating or speaking. At night they took 100-pound (45 kg) sacks of beans and potatoes from the nearby fields and hauled them back to Popowa Yama's entrance, where the younger boys and women were waiting to drag them inside.

In early November, the first signs of winter appeared quickly across the western Ukraine. Long gray stratus clouds stretched across the sky overhead, and the wind blew colder across the prairie. Underground, with

The Nazis remained relentless and ruthless in their search for any sign of escaping Jews.

enough food and fuel for several months, the Jews moved a massive boulder in front of the entrance shaft and barricaded it shut with logs.

During the late days of autumn, the Stermers and their neighbors had been going about the business of staying alive with only a peripheral awareness of what was happening in the world above them. It had been over four months since the entrance to the cave had been filled in by peasants, and with winter quickly approaching, they were confident that Popowa Yama would be abandoned until spring. Yet, unbeknownst to any one of the survivors, the local Ukrainian police had been watching the sinkhole from the nearby woods—and waiting.

"That was a very, very close call," Shlomo said gravely, beginning the story, "We were lucky to survive."

Nissel, Shulim, and their father Zeida had spent the previous day hiding in the barn of a peasant named Semen Sawkie, who, like Munko, was an old family friend and had faithfully sold the Stermers supplies throughout the war. At just past sunset on November 10th, the men helped Sawkie load his wagon with sacks of food and fuel and rode with the peasant to the forest adjacent to the Priest's Grotto as planned.

When the men reached the edge of the woods, Nissel and Shulim jumped down from the wagon and crawled on their stomachs toward the edge of the sinkhole, lifting their heads above

While the cave dwellers kept themselves in a state of semi hibernation for the winter months, the Nazi soldiers did not let the Ukrainian winter snow affect their search for escaping Jews.

the cold, wet grass to see if anyone had watched them approach. The two brothers then slipped down the entrance shaft and returned with Shlomo to the edge of the forest to collect their supplies. As another group of men waited to go outside, the three brothers began pulling the sacks into the cave from underneath.

"But one of the sacks got stuck," Shulim exclaimed suddenly, shoving his shoulder against an imaginary obstacle in front of him. "And the entrance was blocked. We pushed and pulled and we soon discovered that we had trapped ourselves inside. No one could get in or out."

After ten more minutes of trying to pull the sack down through the entrance, the men who had been waiting to go outside started to grow impatient. Then, suddenly, they all heard the sound of footsteps above them.

" 'Who's outside?!' " someone yelled, "We're all here so 'Who's outside?!' " Shulim leaned forward across the table as he spoke and pounded an imaginary door.

The next thing Shulim and Shlomo remember hearing was the sound of gunfire, followed by a barrage of bullets that ricocheted down the shaft and into the cave through the narrow opening.

"WE WERE CONTINUING OUR ROUTINE IN THE CAVE, washing, grinding flour, and preparing our meager meals. We would chop up the wood in small pieces and divide them among our people, making sure that no one used more than he had to."

ABOVE LEFT: A 6-inch (15 cm) railroad spike was the survivors' most important tool, allowing them to shape shoes and other utensils from wood collected from the forest nearby.

ABOVE RIGHT: The survivors' millstone sits on its base, which was carved by Shulim with nothing more than the railroad spike at left.

Instinctively, the men took cover behind the boulders that they used to blockade the entrance. They had no weapons or ammunition, and other than barring entry to the bottom of the shaft, they were helpless against a full-scale assault.

But after the initial round of gunfire, the survivors never heard another shot. Local peasants who gathered around the sinkhole in the aftermath of the attack told the Ukrainian police that the Jews had secret exits all over the place and that it would be impossible to locate every one of them. Over the next few days, the officers swept the fields looking for another way into the cave but found nothing.

"If that sack didn't get stuck, we wouldn't be here," Shulim finally said, "Or maybe it would have been the other guys. You never know. . . . It was one of many miracles."

By early December, the first heavy snows began to fall across the western Ukraine, and the bottom of the Popowa Yama quickly drifted over. Deep underground, the Jews' battle for survival was becoming a war of attrition.

"We were continuing our routine in the cave," Esther wrote as the long winter days wore on, "Washing, grinding flour, and preparing our meager meals. We would chop up the wood in small pieces and divide them among our people, making sure that no one used more than he had to."

Beyond this point in the Stermers' story—after more than 205 days underground—there's nothing in the breadth of human experience to re-create what the survivors endured in Popowa Yama. By this time in his own experiment, Siffre was already back in France, celebrating his new world record over

Nicola measures what was once a bedpost in the survivors' sleeping quarters inside of Priest's Grotto. The Jews usually slept two to three in a bed to share blankets and conserve body heat in the drafty passageways.

Brie and Bordeaux and suffering from psychological wounds he couldn't understand.

When the Stermers talk about their own experiences, however, they refuse to dwell on the conflicts that must have arisen among and between families during those long, difficult months. Physically, many of the survivors already had dwindled to two-thirds of their normal weight. They slept in groups to conserve body heat, condensation soaked their threadbare clothing, and the women sucked on raw potatoes to further stretch their limited supplies.

Yet, throughout their ordeal, it was more than just physical courage and endurance that kept the group alive; it was loyalty and unity. In this way, the Stermers' story is fundamentally different from those of people such as Antarctic explorer Ernest Shackleton. These Jews weren't "survivors" in the Hollywood sense of the word. These were gracious, humble men and women who had outfoxed the Nazis at the peak of their power and survived underground for longer than anyone else in history because, united against a common oppressor, their will to live was unshakable.

"It was our passion to see the complete destruction of the Germans that impelled us to these efforts," Esther wrote. "We told each other that God had Himself created this grotto for us, so that we might live to see the redemptive day of Hitler's downfall."

"We told each other that God had Himself created this grotto for us, SO THAT WE MIGHT LIVE TO SEE THE REDEMPTIVE DAY OF HITLER'S DOWNFALL."

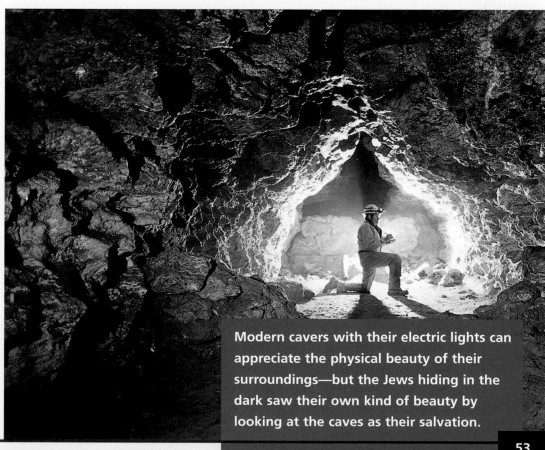

Modern cavers with their electric lights can appreciate the physical beauty of their surroundings—but the Jews hiding in the dark saw their own kind of beauty by looking at the caves as their salvation.

By the end of their third and last day underground,

Nicola and Taylor have been awake for over forty hours, running only on intermittent naps. Thanks in large part to their guides' agility at moving in small spaces, they'd mapped and inventoried all four of Khatki's main rooms and carefully photographed each one of the Jews' artifacts to show to the Stermers back in Montreal.

At five in the afternoon, Sergey appears in the entry room after a two-hour "solo," informing them that he's rediscovered a room a half mile (.8 km) from Khatki that has graffiti written on the walls in Polish and if they hurry, they can get there and back in time to make their rendezvous with their support team on the surface at ten that evening.

Taylor, Nicola, and Sasha reach the room ten minutes later and find Sergey kneeling under a large crack between two sheets of bedrock. He watches the others duckwalk clumsily into the room and then rolls his face skyward, sending a curtain of soft, orange light across the ceiling above him where there are at least ten different inscriptions scrawled into the stone.

The first inscriptions Nicola and Taylor see are written in Ukrainian, with one as recent as 2000. The others are the names of various local cavers who first explored this region of the cave some forty years ago.

Then, suddenly, Taylor hears Nicola whisper, "Oh, my God!"

Directly above him, written in charcoal into the ceiling's delicate crystals, are four words: "Stermer," "Salomon," "Dodyk," and "K.Kurz." Two feet (.6 m) farther down the ceiling toward the wall is the date "1943." (Sol and Shulim chose the name of Esther's father, Salomon, after whom they were both named.)

Nicola and Taylor look at each other speechless. During five separate visits to Montreal, neither Shulim, Shlomo, nor any of their relatives ever mentioned anything about writing their names on the walls. Yet, as cavers, Nicola and Taylor are fully mindful of the significance of their discovery. The unique thing about caves compared with other natural ecosystems is the way history survives underground, almost as if in a

Still in awe at what the expedition has discovered, Chris Nicola examines the survivors' names scrawled into Priest's Grotto's crystalline ceiling in a remote room. The date 1943 is written at the bottom of the ceiling, closest to the entrance.

vacuum, until the first rays of light bring even the smallest details back to life. In its purest form, this is what cave explorers aspire to do when they push virgin passages, and what Nicola had always hoped our expedition would be to the Stermers' story: a revelation of truth.

At just past sunset, after hastily disassembling their camp, the expedition team arrives at the bottom of the entrance shaft dragging all of their equipment through the mud. Even after just seventy-two hours underground, the anticipation of feeling the wind and smelling the earth is overpowering. Sergey throws open the steel door at the top of the entrance shaft, and the passageway where Nicola and Taylor are waiting at the bottom fills instantly with warm, fresh air.

reports began to filter in that the German front was collapsing and Russian troops were approaching. Munko Lubudzin told the Stermer men that he could hear the distant echo of machine-gun fire and see bright orange explosions over the eastern hills at night.

Underground, the survivors greeted the news of their potential liberation with an unsettling mixture of elation and dread. Overhead, the front passed back and forth over the entrance to the sinkhole in a relentless volley of artillery and small arms fire, but beneath 70 feet (21 m) of solid bedrock, the Jews had no way of knowing when it was safe to come out. For the next two weeks, the Stermers and their neighbors waited for news, scarcely daring to eat or sleep.

"Our men would return to us underground upset and confused," Esther wrote of the weeks leading up to her family's liberation. "Their joy was great, but there was also anxiety whether help would reach us, or whether ours would be like the story of Moses, who saw the Promised Land from the distance but was not privileged himself to set foot on it. Might not the same happen to us?"

Finally, one morning in early April, Shlomo approached the bottom of the entrance shaft and saw a small bottle in the mud. The message in the bottle, dropped by their friend Munko, read simply: "The Germans are already gone."

Ten days later, on April 12, 1944, the Stermers and their neighbors stashed their tools and supplies deep inside the cave, wrestled on their clothes, and squeezed one by one out through Popowa Yama's narrow entrance. Heavy snow had fallen over the previous week, and dirty, slushy water flowed into the shaft from above, covering all of them with ice and mud. Outside the entrance, they scaled the steep banks of the sinkhole and rose to stand into the blinding sunshine for the first time in 344 days. In the distance, the road to Korolowka was littered with burned-out German tanks and machinery, but for Esther and her family, the sight of their war-torn homeland was one of the most beautiful things they had ever seen.

Nissel Stermer

"For years daylight had frightened us," Esther wrote. "It was only nights and in the dark that we had felt secure. For years we had hidden in bunkers, caves and other dark places, and had been afraid to be seen in God's world. Now we were all able to walk in the middle of the day outdoors . . . Salvation had come."

Sixty years later, in the quiet afternoon light of Shulim's living room back in Montreal, the survivors recounted their memories of their liberation with repose and humility. Shulim was quiet for the first time since we started talking over five hours ago, and across from him, Shlomo simply nodded his head and said repeatedly, "It was a beautiful, beautiful day."

"For my own part, I don't think I could have lasted any longer from the time that we were liberated," Pepkale said softly when it came her turn to speak.

"By the time that I came out of the cave, I had forgotten what the sun was. And when we came out the sun must have been shining. . . . I told my mother, I said 'Close the candle! Turn out the light!'

"FOR YEARS DAYLIGHT HAD FRIGHTENED US. . . . For years we had hidden in bunkers, caves and other dark places, and had been afraid to be seen in God's world. Now we were all able to walk in the middle of the day outdoors. . . . SALVATION HAD COME."

LEFT TO RIGHT: Pepkale Dodyk, Ekta Katz, Shulim Stermer, Shlomo Stermer, Sol Wexler, and Shunkale Hochman (previously Dodyk)

I couldn't believe it. I had forgotten completely what the sun was."

At the top of the sinkhole, the Stermers stood motionless, letting their eyes adjust to the bright, white light. When they were finally able to focus, they could barely recognize one another. Their faces were jaundiced and malnourished, their clothes were tattered, and their skin was caked in thick, yellow mud. Their town of Korolowka was almost completely destroyed. Of more than fourteen thousand Jews that lived in the region before World War II, only three hundred had survived.

In the chaos that followed the Russians' liberation of the Ukraine, the Stermers didn't wait around for justice. They abandoned Korolowka forever in June 1945 with only the jewelry sewn into their boots, finally arriving at a displaced persons camp in Fernwald, Germany, in November. They were assigned to a group of small bunks in a large room and spent the next four weeks eating, showering, and sleeping securely for

ABOVE: Esther Stermer *(right)* **and her sister Shancie Kimelman at the displaced persons camp at Fernwald, 1946.**

RIGHT: The Allied liberators were greeted with joy and thanksgiving as they moved through the region, freeing ill-treated emaciated prisoners.

the first time in more than half a decade. Family photos from that period show the survivors dressed in tailored shirts and jackets and posing defiantly, as if nothing in the world could defeat them.

Today, the Stermers' survival in Verteba and Popowa Yama still shapes everything about their lives. Some, like Pepkale, still travel with small stashes of food to safeguard against the possibility of going hungry. Overall, the survivors remain devoutly religious, both in spite and because of their experiences underground. When Nicola and I asked if the Stermers felt they were blessed to survive, however, Shulim and Shlomo were quickly dismissive of the notion that divine intervention had played a role in their triumph. God remains a controversial protagonist for almost every Holocaust survivor. But in the Stermers' case specifically, attributing their survival to a higher power takes some of the magic away from their story. It understates their resolve and the heart-pounding courage it took to fight for every day they stayed alive.

"We were masters of our own fate in the cave," Esther wrote at the end of her memoir, "There was no one to whom we owed our safety or upon whom we depended. After our men came in from the outside and scraped off the mud which would cling to their clothing as they slid through the entrance, and they had washed, they were free men."

"WE WERE MASTERS OF OUR OWN FATE IN THE CAVE. There was no one to whom we owed our safety or upon whom we depended. After our men came in from the outside and scraped off the mud which would cling to their clothing as they slid through the entrance, and they had washed, THEY WERE FREE MEN."

The Stermer clan after their liberation at Fernwald DP camp (*back row from left*): Shulim Stermer, Chana Richter, Joseph Richter, Etka Katz, Abe Katz, and Shlomo Stermer. Front row from left: Shulim's wife Czarna, Esther Stermer, Henia Dodyk, and her daughter Pepkale.

As NICOLA AND TAYLOR PACKED UP TO LEAVE, they felt uplifted. In the course of that afternoon, they had discovered that the heart of the Stermers' story was more than just survival. It was a story about loyalty, persistence, ingenuity, faith, and hope. And because no one could take those things away from them, the Stermers and their neighbors had accomplished what most Holocaust survivors could never even imagine: they had become masters of their own destinies.

"When we get together like this and I see the grandchildren," Shulim said as we rose to leave, "I see the family and it's an affair and I see nice kids. . . . And I say to myself, 'It was worth the fight to survive.'"

Shulim then paused briefly, looking down at a copy of his mother's memoir lying on the table in front of him.

"Like my mother said,"
he repeated quietly,
"We will fight to survive."

"When we get together like this and I see the grandchildren, I see the family and it's an affair and I see nice kids... And I say to myself, 'It was worth the fight to survive.'"

The Stermer family including Nissel's wife Pearl, Shulim, Shlomo, Yetta, Chana, Henia, and Etka with their spouses, their children, and their grandchildren.

1922
Esther's family *(left to right)*: Nissel, Esther's husband Zeida, holding Shulim, Esther, Chana and Henia. Etka and Shlomo were not born yet.

1942
An order is given that the town of Korolowka must become "clean of Jews."

Stermer family and friends go to Verteba cave.

September 1939
Germany invades Poland, beginning World War II.

1910
Esther Stermer moved to Korolowka when she married. Her children were born there, and they lived a happy and prosperous life until the Nazis arrived.

1936
A Stermer family portrait *(left to right)* Standing: Nissel, Chana, Shlomo, Shulim, Esther's son-in-law Fishel, and Etka. Sitting: Esther, her husband Zeida, Henia and Pepkale

May 5, 1943
Stermer family and friends enter Priest's Grotto.

April 12, 1944
Stermers and friends emerge from Priest's Grotto.

May 7, 1945
Germany stops fighting and surrenders all forces.

December 1949
Family members cross the Atlantic to begin new lives in the United States and Canada.

1946
Family members arrive at the Fernwald, Germany displaced persons camp.

December 2002

Sol Wexler contacts Chris Nicola and the quest to unravel The Secret of Priest's Grotto *begins.*

AFTERWORD

The release of Peter Lane Taylor's article in *National Geographic Adventure* in June 2004 generated international media attention, including segments on *The Today Show*, National Public Radio, the BBC, and ABC (Australian Broadcasting Company) Radio.

This press, in turn, brought other Priest Grotto survivors who had left the Ukraine shortly after the end of World War II to Nicola's attention, many of whom hadn't seen one another in almost six decades. Among them were Ulo Barad, the young boy who was brought into the cave and nursed back to health by Etka Dodyk; Norman Kittner, who was two years old inside of Priest's Grotto; Dorothy Karpf, who was nine; Karl (Ziundi) Kurz, who now lives in Israel; Daniel Goldberg, who eventually joined the Russian army; Luzer Reibel; Fradel Kittner; and Mariya Gritsiv, who runs an adoption agency in Georgia. Nicola also eventually made contact with Mundik (Marvin) Reible.

Today, a total of fourteen of the cave dwellers from Priest's Grotto are alive and well, living in the United States, Canada, and Israel. Saul Stermer, who shares the oldest living survivor record with Fradel Kittner, is currently eighty-six. Nissel Stermer sadly passed away from Parkinson's disease just two years before Taylor and Nicola first visited Montreal in 2003.

Chris Nicola continues to travel around the country lecturing about the Priest's Grotto story and the Holocaust and has spoken at many synagogues. He has also returned to the Ukraine and Priest's Grotto several times since his historic expedition with Taylor in 2003. On these expeditions, Nicola's teams have discovered more artifacts, interviewed additional firsthand witnesses to the survivors' story, and uncovered new archives and research providing key historical context to what the survivors accomplished. Nicola's efforts are also ensuring that Priest's Grotto and Khatki will be protected permanently and that the survivors' artifacts still in the cave are properly preserved. In August of 2006, Nicola's team escorted the descendents of various survivors back into the historic area of the cave for the first time and conducted diving surveys in Priest's Grotto's lakes to search for additional artifacts.

The story of what happened in Priest's Grotto and Chris Nicola's search for the last living survivors is being developed into a motion picture and television documentary.